T0171021

Copyright © 2019 James Stone.

All rights reserved. No part of this book may be used or reproduced by any means, graphic, electronic, or mechanical, including photocopying, recording, taping or by any information storage retrieval system without the written permission of the author except in the case of brief quotations embodied in critical articles and reviews.

Archway Publishing books may be ordered through booksellers or by contacting:

Archway Publishing
1663 Liberty Drive
Bloomington, IN 47403
www.archwaypublishing.com
1 (888) 242-5904

Because of the dynamic nature of the Internet, any web addresses or links contained in this book may have changed since publication and may no longer be valid. The views expressed in this work are solely those of the author and do not necessarily reflect the views of the publisher, and the publisher hereby disclaims any responsibility for them.

Any people depicted in stock imagery provided by Getty Images are models, and such images are being used for illustrative purposes only.
Certain stock imagery © Getty Images.

ISBN: 978-1-4808-6661-4 (hc)

Print information available on the last page.

Archway Publishing rev. date: 2/13/2019

Night Night Dance

A CLASSIC LULLABY

A Family's Wish

By James Stone

In The Beginning

Family's Surname

_____

Mother's Given Name _____

Father's Given Name _____

Child's Given Name

_____

Date of Birth _____

Place Of Birth _____

Length _____

Weight _____

Colors of Eyes _____

Color of Hair _____

Night Night Dance
A Classic Lullaby
A Family's Wish

James Stone

Night Night Dance

100 bpm

Piano

1 Night night dance 2 Night night dance 3 Time to do the

4 night night dance 5 Go to sleep 6 not a peep 7 Time to do the

8 night night dance 9 Night night dance 10 Night night dance 11 Time to do the

12 night night dance 13 Momm -y's here 14 Dadd -y's here 15 With you as you 16 sleep

17 Night night dance 18 Night night dance 19 Time to do the 20 Night night dance

21 Soft kisses and 22 pleas -ant 23 dreams will be 24 here when you a -wake 25 We will be

26 here with you 27 al - 28 ways

Night Night Dance

Night Night Dance

Time to do The Night Night Dance

Go to Sleep not a Peep

Time to do The Night Night Dance

Night Night Dance

Night Night Dance

Time to do The Night Night Dance

Mommy's Here

Daddy's Here

With you as you Sleep

Night Night Dance

Night Night Dance

Time to do The Night Night Dance

Soft Kisses and Pleasant Dreams

We Will be Here with You Always

Weekly Experiences

1st

2nd

3rd

4th

5th

6th

7th

8th

9th

10th

11th

12th

13th

14th

15th

16th

17th

18th

19th

20th

21st

22nd

23rd

24th

25th

26th

27th

28th

29th

30th

31st

32nd

33rd

34th

35th

36th

37th

38th

39th

40th

41st

42nd

43rd

44th

45th

46th

47th

48th

49th

50th

51st

52nd Birthday